RUBANK EDUCATIONAL
LIBRARY No. 295

ONLINE MEDIA INCLUDED
Audio Recordings
Printable Piano Accompaniments

Concert and Contest COLLECTION

for

FRENCH HORN

Compiled and Edited

by **H. VOXMAN**

PLAYBACK+
Speed · Pitch · Balance · Loop

To access recordings and PDF accompaniments visit:
www.halleonard.com/mylibrary

Enter Code
7177-9967-9506-5389

ISBN 978-1-4234-7723-5

7777 W. BLUEMOUND RD. P.O. BOX 13819 MILWAUKEE, WI 53213

Visit Hal Leonard Online at
www.halleonard.com

Prelude

from Act III of Hérodiade

French Horn (in F)

JULES MASSENET
Transcribed by H. Voxman

Allerseelen

French Horn (in F)

RICHARD STRAUSS, Op. 10, No. 8
Transcribed by H. Voxman

Tranquillo

Ballade

French Horn (in F)

LEROY OSTRANSKY

Andante cantabile

Scherzo

French Horn (in F)

V. SHELUKOV
Transcribed by H. Voxman

Mélodie

French Horn (in F)

CLÉMENT LENOM
Edited by H. Voxman

Farewell Serenade

French Horn (in F)

W. HERFURTH, Op. 85
Edited by H. Voxman

Andante con moto

Nocturne

from A Midsummer Night's Dream

French Horn (in F)

F. MENDELSSOHN
Transcribed by H. Voxman

*For shorter performance cut from * to *

Vocalise

French Horn (in F)

SERGEI RACHMANINOFF
Transcribed by H. Voxman

Lentamente. Molto cantabile

Two Outdoor Scenes

French Horn (in F)

LEROY OSTRANSKY

Romance

French Horn (in F)

C. SAINT-SAËNS, Op. 36
Edited by H. Voxman

* more animated

Rêverie

French Horn (in F)

ALEXANDRE GLAZOUNOW, Op. 24
Edited by H. Voxman

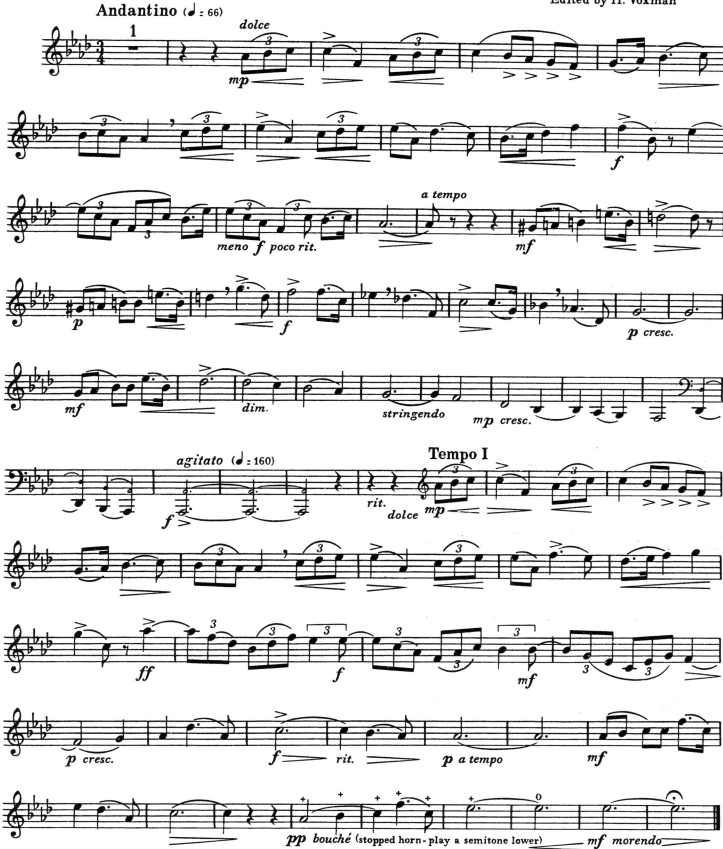

La Chasse

French Horn (in F)

PAUL KOEPKE

Romanza and Rondo

from Concerto No. 4, K. 495

French Horn (in F)

W. A. MOZART
Edited by H. Voxman

RONDO
Allegro vivace

Le Cor
(The Horn)

French Horn (in F)

ANGE FLÉGIER
Transcribed by H. Voxman